THE ADVENTURES OF HUCKLEBERRY FINN

Artists: Penko Gelev
Sotir Gelev

Editor: Stephen Haynes
Editorial Assistant: Mark Williams

Published in Great Britain in 2008 by
Book House, an imprint of
The Salariya Book Company Ltd
25 Marlborough Place, Brighton, BNI IUB
www.salariya.com
www.book-house.co.uk

ISBN-13: 978-1-906370-07-7 (PB)

SALARIYA

1 3 5 7 9 8 6 4 2

A CIP catalogue record for this book is available
from the British Library.

Printed and bound in China.
Printed on paper from sustainable sources.

Visit our website at **www.salariya.com**
for **free** electronic versions of:
You Wouldn't Want to be an Egyptian Mummy!
You Wouldn't Want to be a Roman Gladiator!
Avoid Joining Shackleton's Polar Expedition!
Avoid Sailing on a 19th-Century Whaling Ship!

Picture credits:
pp. 40, 41, 43 (riverboats) © 2003 Topham Picturepoint/TopFoto.co.uk
p. 43 (map) Carolyn Franklin
p. 47 HIP/TopFoto.co.uk; photo Peter H. Hunt
Every effort has been made to trace copyright holders. The Salariya Book Company apologises for any omissions and would be pleased, in such cases, to add an acknowledgement in future editions.

THE ADVENTURES OF
A HUCKLEBERRY FINN

GRAFFEX™

MARK TWAIN

Illustrated by

Penko Gelev

BOOK HOUSE

Retold by

Tom Ratliff

Series created and designed by

David Salariya

You don't know about me, without you have read a book by the name of *The Adventures of Tom Sawyer*, but that ain't no matter. That book was made by Mr Mark Twain, and he told the truth, mainly. There was things which he stretched… but I never seen anybody but lied, one time or another…

CHARACTERS

Huckleberry Finn

Tom Sawyer

Jim

Miss Watson

Judge Thatcher

Widow Douglas

Pap Finn

The King

The Duke

Mary Jane Wilks

Susan Wilks

Joanna Wilks

Silas Phelps

Sally Phelps

Aunt Polly

CIVILISING HUCK

The Mississippi Valley, c.1840

In case you haven't read *Tom Sawyer*...

Tom and I found a treasure chest full of gold. We split the money equally, and since I was practically an orphan[1] Judge Thatcher looked after my share.

Now let me tell you what happened next...

The Widow Douglas took me in as her son. She was nice enough, and even bought me some new clothes, but I wasn't used to living in a house all the time.

We are all sinners.

For one thing, she was religious. Every night the Widow would read to me from the Bible and then she would pray for me.

Don't scrunch up like that, Huckleberry.

The Widow's sister, Miss Watson, would nag me about every little thing until I could hardly stand it.

You gotta join up with us, Huck.

Tom Sawyer was always looking for adventure, and one night he told me that he wanted to start a band of robbers.

He'll think it was witches...

...or a ghost.

Tom and I found ways to have fun, like playing tricks on Jim, Miss Watson's slave.[2] One night we stole his hat and put it in a tree.

Anyone here who betrays us will have his throat cut!

Tom found an old cave near the river, and the gang met there late one night. We took a blood oath never to tell our secrets.

---

1. practically an orphan: Huck's father is still alive, but Huck rarely sees him.
2. Miss Watson's slave: Slavery was allowed in some American states until 1865.

LIFE WITH THE WIDOW

Uh-oh!

When I got back to the Widow's that night, I discovered my new clothes were stained with mud.

You don't appreciate all we do for you.

Miss Watson yelled at me, but the Widow just washed my clothes and never even asked how I got them so dirty. I was grateful for that.

A boy like you is nothing but trouble. Why in my day...

I liked the Widow, though Miss Watson was more than I could bear. I considered running off – I missed the freedom of living on my own.

You're safer with the Widow.

I'll teach you to respect your elders!

But if I left, I ran the risk of running into my Pap. I hadn't seen him in over a year, but he'd soon show up if he heard about my money. Pap used to beat me.

It might be old man Finn.

When a bloated body turned up in the river one day, some thought it might be Pap, but I decided to stay put until I knew for sure he was gone.

Tom planned to attack a caravan of merchants...

Fight to the death, men! No prisoners!

...but it turned out to be a Sunday-school picnic!

Six times seven is thirty-five, ma'am.

I was getting used to being in school and even started to like it. It was winter – too cold to live outside – and I was learning to spell and read and multiply.

When I got tired of school I played hooky, but living with the Widow wasn't that bad. I liked knowing where my next meal was coming from, and I was even getting used to sleeping in a bed.

What a mess you are always making!

But Miss Watson was always after me.

There's only one person who cuts his boot like that.

One morning I found boot prints in the snow. There was a cross in one heel to keep away the devil.

My Pap was in town!

Your money is perfectly safe, Huck.

I had to get rid of my money any way I could! I tried to give it to Judge Thatcher, but he told me not to worry. He even gave me a dollar.

You gotta be careful 'round him.

Miss Watson's slave Jim had a hairball[1] and could predict the future. He said that Pap had two angels hovering around him – a good and a bad one.

Well, it's about time you showed up.

When I got home and lit my candle, there was Pap in my room!

1. hairball: a ball of hair and wax. Superstitious people once believed that this could have magic powers.

PAP

He had climbed up on the shed and in through the window.

I wasn't scared, but I had to be careful or he would wallop me – so I kept my mouth shut and waited for him to speak his mind.

What made him maddest was that I'd been going to school. He shoved a book in my face and asked if I could read it. I didn't want to, but a part of me was proud that I could, so I began to read.

I didn't get more than a few sentences out before Pap snatched the book from my hands.

Pap finally got around to the real reason for his visit.

He said if I knew what was good for me, I would hand over the money.

He searched my pockets and found the dollar the Judge had given me.

Next day Pap went to see the Judge. He was drunk and threatened the Judge, but it didn't go any good.

Judge Thatcher and Widow Douglas tried to get custody of me,[1] but the court was reluctant to take me away from Pap.

Pap came back to see me. He was so mad that I gave him $3 I had hidden away, just to get rid of him. He used the money to get drunk for a week.

One day Pap saw me heading for school, and gave me a really bad beating. I didn't like school all that much, but I kept going just to spite him. I figured anything that Pap hated couldn't be all bad.

1. get custody of me: become my legal guardians instead of Pap.

PAP KIDNAPS ME

Pap was afraid that the Widow would win her court case, so he took me across the river to an abandoned log hut.

I was free to roam around during the day, but at night Pap locked the door so I couldn't escape. He even slept with the key in his pocket.

Pap had an old gun that he stole. We fished and hunted, and he sold the fish for liquor. The Widow sent someone to rescue me, but Pap drove him off.

I got used to the lifestyle: I didn't have to wash too often, or eat from a plate. But Pap was still Pap, and I got tired of the beatings.

One night I found a rusty old saw blade. I hid it away and waited until Pap went off across the river.

The boards were thick and it took a long time to saw through. I was careful to clean up the sawdust so Pap wouldn't know what I was up to.

When he came back, Pap said the Widow was going to get custody of me. I didn't like the idea of going back to her, but I couldn't stay with Pap much longer either.

I knew Pap would kill me rather than let me go. I had to get out of there before it was too late!

I gotta set out on my own so no-one can ever find me.

The money's mine! That durned Judge and that Widow ain't gonna get it.

Pap had brought back a load of supplies. I unloaded the skiff[1] while he drank the whisky he'd bought.

I was between two worlds – I had to get away from Pap but hated the idea of going back to the Widow's.

I waited for Pap to pass out. But the more he drank, the more agitated he got, ranting on about the Judge, and the Widow, and the money. In the end I fell asleep before he did.

Snakes! Get 'em off me!

Someone was trying to break in!

When I woke up Pap was screaming. He was so drunk, he imagined snakes were attacking him. He pulled out a knife and said he was going to kill me, but he was too drunk and soon dozed off again.

I got his gun and laid it across the turnip barrel, pointing at him, just in case. When he woke up he grabbed the gun and asked what I was doing. I told the first lie that popped into my head.

I went out to check the fishing lines.

I can put this to good use!

Logs were floating by from the sawmills upstream. Then a canoe came along! I was so excited that I jumped in and pulled it to shore. Pap would have sold it – it was worth $10 – but I hid it, hoping to use it for my escape.

1. skiff: small rowing boat.

13

MY CLEVER ESCAPE

When Pap woke up he was still in a bad mood. I stayed out of his way, and offered to cook him some catfish for breakfast.

We found some logs tied together and pulled them ashore. Then Pap locked me in the cabin and set off across the river to sell the logs.

This was my chance! I finished sawing my way out. I was free!

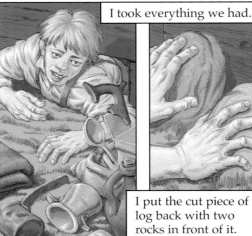

I put the cut piece of log back with two rocks in front of it.

...and dragged it back to the cabin.

Then I smashed in the door.

I cut the hog's throat and let it bleed on the floor, then dragged the carcass to the river and threw it in.

I pulled out some of my hair, dipped the axe in hog blood and stuck the hair to the blade.

As I paddled downriver, I hoped that Pap would be fooled by my tricks. But I didn't care. I had escaped, and for the first time in my life I felt truly free.

Somebody's drowned for sure.

It worked!

I tied up at Jackson's Island, about 12 miles downriver. A passing ferry boat was shooting a cannon – which was supposed to make a dead body rise to the surface.

From my hiding place I could see everyone on the ferry: Judge Thatcher, the Widow, Tom Sawyer, Pap, and Tom's Aunt Polly. They all thought I was dead! I felt bad in a way, but I was so happy to be free that I didn't care.

Sure is lonesome here.

What if it's Pap come looking for me?

After that I set up camp on the island. I made a tent out of blankets and caught a catfish for supper. For a few days I really loved my freedom, but after a while I started to wish I had some company.

One day I stumbled upon a smouldering campfire. I was not alone! I was so scared, I hid in a tree.

I stayed there two hours, my heart pounding.

Jim!

You're dead, Huck!

Your ghost has come back to haunt me.

I ain't dead, Jim. It was all a trick.

When I calmed down I hiked back to where the campfire was. To my surprise, there was someone sleeping near the fire – it was Miss Watson's slave!

He was terrified.

It took a while to convince Jim that I wasn't dead. It wasn't until I got out some bacon and cooked us breakfast that he finally calmed down.

THE TWO RUNAWAYS

Jim had run away the night he heard I was killed. He hadn't brought any food with him and had been living on wild berries.

I told Jim how I had faked my death. Now I was rid of Pap and the Widow and the money!

I asked Jim why he had run away. He had a family, and I knew that Miss Watson treated him well.

Jim said that Miss Watson wanted to sell him downriver in New Orleans for $800. That's why he ran off.

His plan was to swim across the river to Illinois, which was a Free State.[1] But it was too far, so he settled for the island.

He was afraid that I would tell someone where he was. I said I wouldn't, and we swore an oath to keep each other's secrets.

This worried me some. I didn't want anyone to know I had helped a slave escape. I had a reputation to uphold, and didn't want to be called an abolitionist.[2] At the same time, I didn't want Jim to get caught.

1. Free State: a state where slavery was not allowed. Once Jim got there, he would be less likely to be caught and sent back.
2. abolitionist: a person who thinks slavery should be abolished (banned). Huck is confused because he has been brought up to believe that slavery is right, but now he is not so sure.

16

It looked like rain, so we moved into a cave Jim had found. For the next several days it poured, and the river rose higher and higher.

When the rain finally stopped, we found the river filled with debris from the flooding. We captured a good-sized raft of logs, and as we were tying it up a whole house came floating by! We paddled out to it in the canoe.

In the house we found some silver coins, a tin lantern, a few girls' dresses, a hatchet, and some candles. In one room Jim made a grim discovery.

We decided to leave the island, but first we had to make sure it was safe. I put on one of the dresses and I took the canoe over to the Illinois side of the river.

I knocked on the first door I came to and a nice woman let me in. She told me it was dangerous for a young girl like me to be out alone at night.

She said that a young man by the name of Huck Finn had been killed by a runaway slave named Jim. Jim hadn't been seen since the night of the murder.

There was a $300 reward for the runaway. Some people believed he was hiding on Jackson's Island!

LIFE ON THE RAFT

I got out of there as fast as I could! When I got back to the island I lit a fire as a decoy while Jim loaded the raft. We set off downriver with the canoe in tow.

It was pretty dark. We tried to stay in the middle of the river to avoid being seen.

At daybreak we tied up to a sandbar and covered the raft with some cottonwood branches.

Jim built a tepee at one end of the raft. He put some dirt down on the floor so we could light a fire to cook our meals and keep us warm on cold nights.

We sailed at night and tied up every morning. It was a pretty good life!

One night we came upon a wrecked steamboat. We decided to investigate, and tied up the raft at one end of the wreck.

As we snuck on board we heard voices. Jim was scared, but I told him we would be all right if we kept quiet.

We found some cigars, a spyglass,[1] and some blankets – but we nearly got caught and only just managed to get away.

I was glad we had escaped, and glad Jim was with me. I was beginning to like him a lot. I was starting to see that he wasn't just a slave but a real person, like me.

18   1. spyglass: a small telescope.

We were headed for Cairo, Illinois, where the Ohio River joins the Mississippi.

But it was pretty foggy and we sailed past Cairo in the dark. Jim was upset but I was secretly relieved.

I worried about Miss Watson, who had put up the $300 reward. I wanted to keep my promise to Jim, but I was feeling guilty about helping a runaway slave.

Jim said once he was free he'd save all his money so he could buy his wife and child. Then they'd all be free.

He said if he couldn't buy them he'd have to steal them. This upset me – my conscience began to bother me some more.[1]

Jim was a good friend, but I was breaking the law by helping him escape. I didn't care about the reward, but the problem weighed heavy on my heart.

I told Jim I had to go ashore. I was planning to turn him in. But as I paddled off, Jim called out to me. His words cut me like a knife.

Suddenly in the dark I saw a small boat coming towards me.

The men in the boat asked who was on the raft. I stuttered a bit and then I lied. Miss Watson was right about me – I was a liar and doomed forever.

1. Huck's conscience: Huck wants his friend to be a free man, but he knows that it is against the law to help a slave escape. His conscience is troubled because in order to do what he thinks is right – to set Jim free – he must break the law.

THE FEUD[1]

It's coming straight for us!

It felt good to be back on the raft, but my joy was short-lived. Suddenly a steamboat appeared through the fog.

The steamer ran over us...

Jim! Jim! Help!

...and the next thing I knew, I was in the water.

I'll tell them I fell off a riverboat.

I swam for shore and walked quite a way before I found a house. It was a large cabin, a nice home that told me the people who lived there were well off.

Oh, you poor thing! You're lucky to be alive.

The Grangerfords were decent people and invited me in. Mrs Grangerford gave me some dry clothes that belonged to her son Buck, who was my age.

Can't beat home cooking!

I had my first home-cooked meal in a month: corn pone,[2] buttermilk, and corned beef.

I hope Jim ain't drowned.

Buck and I became friends and we had fun hunting and fishing. But from time to time I wondered what had happened to Jim – was he still alive?

It's my duty to kill Shepherdsons, even if I get killed too.

Buck told me there was a feud between his family and the Shepherdson family. Several members of both families had been killed in the feud.

I liked living with the Grangerfords; they were nice to me. They were so rich that each person had their own servant. I was given a slave named Jack, which made me feel a bit funny, as he reminded me a little of Jim.

1. feud: a long-running quarrel between two families; a vendetta.
2. corn pone: bread made from corn (maize).

One day when Buck and I were out hunting we met a rider coming our way. It was one of the Shepherdsons! Buck shot at him, but missed.

We ran off, and I half expected to feel bullets go flying past my head, but Harney never fired at us.

The next morning we went to church. The Grangerfords brought their rifles, and when the Shepherdsons arrived, they had their weapons too.

I expected that after church there would be a shoot-out, but it didn't happen. When the service was over we went home and had a delicious Sunday dinner.

After dinner, Buck's sister, Miss Sophia, took me aside. She had left her Bible at the church; would I get it for her? I ran there and back as fast as I could.

When I gave her the Bible, she thanked me. Then she pulled a small slip of paper from between the pages.

Soon after, Miss Sophia ran off with Harney Shepherdson! That slip of paper must have been a secret message.

We went after the Shepherdsons and there was a terrible gun battle. Buck was hit, and fell into the river.

Buck was dead! The whole thing seemed so senseless to me. I set out alone, hoping to find Jim.

THE DUKE AND THE KING

Praise the Lord! You're alive!

It's good to be back home on the raft again.

Jim was overjoyed to see me. He was sure I had drowned, and for the second time I had to convince him that I wasn't dead.

We got back into our old ways, travelling at night and sleeping during the day. I was beginning to think of the raft as home, and I was happy that I hadn't turned Jim in. I didn't care about my reputation any more – Jim was my friend and I had to protect him.

These two are trouble, for sure.

What a cosy little raft you have here.

One night when I went ashore I met two men who were running for their lives, with dogs close on their heels. Before I could react, they jumped into our canoe.

The younger man sold fake patent medicines – what Pap called 'snake oil'. The older man worked scams at temperance shows.[1] Oddly enough, they didn't seem to know each other.

I've made a fortune in my day.

They began bragging about their cons.[2] The young man claimed to be an actor, a hypnotist, a singing teacher and a phrenologist.[3] The older man specialised in running camp meetings,[4] telling fortunes, doctoring, and even preaching.

I could tell these two were crooked – the lazy sort that preferred cheating people to doing an honest day's work. They were going to cause us a lot of trouble if we weren't careful.

1. temperance shows: public meetings to persuade people to give up drinking alcohol.
2. cons: tricks, swindles.
3. phrenologist: a person who claims to be able to tell another person's character by feeling the shape of their head.
4. camp meetings: religious meetings held in a tent or in the open air (see page 24).

The younger man claimed to be the Duke of Bridgewater.

The older man went one better, claiming to be the rightful heir to the throne of France.

Since he would be King one day, he said we should treat him with proper respect at all times.

I could see that the Duke was feeling bested, until the King suddenly remembered that his father knew the Duke's ancestors. This made both men happy.

They were obviously frauds and liars, but I could see we would have to put up with them for a while.

The Duke asked me why we were travelling at night. I told him that I was afraid someone might try to steal Jim.

The Duke and the King took over the tepee, and argued over which of them should get Jim's bed, made of corn shucks, or mine, which was made of straw.

That night there was a terrible rainstorm. With the tepee occupied, I slept outside. When a large wave washed over the side of the raft, I got soaked and Jim had a good laugh over my misfortune.

1. takes precedence: comes first.

THE FRAUDSTERS AT WORK

One morning we stopped near the small village of Pokeville. The Duke spotted a printing shop. The King and I found a camp meeting on the edge of town.

At least a thousand people were crammed in to hear the preacher speak.

The King jumped up and announced that he was a pirate, making his living by robbing people. But by some miracle the camp meeting had reformed him and he was no longer a sinner.

The crowd was so moved that they took up a collection for the King. He made over $87 – and he managed to steal three jugs of whisky too.

In the meantime the Duke had made $9.50 conning[1] people at the print shop. He was impressed that the King had made so much at the camp meeting.

The Duke had printed a handbill saying that Jim was a runaway slave. If anyone asked questions, we could tie him up and pretend we'd captured him.

Jim didn't trust those two frauds, and neither did I. But we were still free, and that was all that mattered.

1. conning: tricking, swindling.
2. rubes: country bumpkins.

At sunrise next morning we didn't tie up. It felt good to keep going.

Next, the frauds decided to put on a play. The King had a trunk full of costumes, and they began practising *Romeo and Juliet*,[1] with the Duke as Juliet.

They also worked on the swordfighting scene from *Richard III*, and tried *Hamlet* and *Macbeth*. They were pretty awful.

When they were ready, the King found a small town and we went ashore. It was our lucky day, said the Duke – a circus was in town and had drawn a huge crowd.

The Duke hired the courthouse to put on the show, and we put up handbills advertising the performance. The ads drew quite a crowd. I began to wonder if the frauds really could make any money in such a small town.

1. *Romeo and Juliet*: All the plays mentioned on this page are by Shakespeare.

SHAKESPEARE

I snuck into the circus.

This is grand!

What light through yonder window breaks?

Later, the frauds put on their Shakespeare show, but it was a flop – only twelve paying customers, and they laughed throughout the performance. Actually, I couldn't blame them – the Duke wasn't much of an actor and it all seemed rather silly.

Show's over. Thank you all for coming.

Is that all?

But the King didn't give up. He printed another playbill for 'The King's Cameleopard: or The Royal Nonesuch – Ladies and children not admitted'. That night the house was packed. The audience howled with laughter as the Duke pranced around.

But the show was very short and the crowd felt cheated.

BOO!

Show's over. Thank you.

Jim! Get ready to shove off!

I thought we were done for – but someone in the crowd said they should tell their friends how good the show was.

They were ashamed of being fooled, and wanted their friends to be fooled as well. So the next night the house was packed again and the same thing happened.

The third night drew the biggest crowd of all. But Jim and I had got the raft ready and we shoved off before anyone was the wiser. The final tally was $465!

AAARGH!

Jim had the idea of putting on one of the King's costumes whenever the rest of us left the raft. If anyone showed up, he would jump about and grunt to scare them off.

This looks promising.

The King took me with him to the Tennessee side of the river to check things out.

Poor Peter Wilks was mighty sick.

A boy told us about a man who lived nearby. The man was dying, and his two brothers were travelling from England to see him one last time.

The whole town is in mourning.

But, sadly, the man had died before his brothers arrived.

England, you say? Hmm.

The older brother, Harvey Wilks, had an estate in England. His younger brother, William, was deaf and dumb.

And you don't have to say a word.

The King reckoned he could do a pretty good English accent and pretend to be Harvey. William would be easy for the Duke, as he wouldn't have to say a thing.

I was given the role of their servant. We flagged down a steamboat and took it to the village where Peter Wilks lived. When we arrived, the King spoke to the first man he saw.

Can you tell me, kind sir, where Peter Wilks lives?

THE ULTIMATE CON TRICK

The townsfolk were overjoyed to meet the long-lost brothers. The Duke kept making these phony hand signs to make people think he was deaf and dumb. It made me ashamed to be a part of the human race.

We met Peter's nieces – Mary Jane, Susan and Joanna – and then we went inside to where the coffin was laid out. The Duke and the King set to crying like you wouldn't believe.

The King gave a tearful speech about how wonderful it was to be welcomed by his brother's friends.

The will[1] was read, revealing that a bag of gold was hidden in the cellar. The frauds retrieved it and promised to give their share of the money to the nieces.

The nieces were overjoyed at their generosity. So were most of the townspeople, who had crowded into the Wilks home to see the visitors from England.

But not everyone was fooled. Dr Robinson accused the King of being an impostor.

The Doctor begged the girls not to trust the fake uncles – but to his dismay, Mary Jane gave the bag of gold to the King to invest for them.

But most people believed the frauds were the real uncles, and the Doctor left in a huff. I wished I could go with him.

1. will: a legal document that gives instructions for what to do with a person's property after their death.

That night I ate in the kitchen with the younger niece, Joanna, and she asked me lots of questions about life in England.

I got to telling lies, and was nearly tripped up as I didn't know the first thing about England.

I was rescued when Mary Jane and Susan came in and took Joanna to task[1] for flustering me. They were so sweet that I began to feel bad about cheating them.

I knew I couldn't let those frauds steal from these girls. I snuck into the King's room...

...but before I could take the gold I heard footsteps in the hall. I hid behind a curtain.

The Duke and the King entered. They were arguing over whether to leave immediately, or stay and sell off the house and land, too.

It was bad enough to steal the gold – but to sell the house and leave the poor girls homeless was more than I could bear. I had to expose the frauds, in spite of the danger to me and Jim.

The King hid the gold under his mattress for safe keeping. Little did he know that I was about to steal it from him!

1. took Joanna to task: told her off.

TELLING THE TRUTH

No-one will think to look in here.

And as we say our final farewell to Peter Wilks...

I crept downstairs with the gold and found Mary Jane in the parlour crying over the body of her Uncle Peter. I had no plan, but the coffin gave me an idea.

After Mary Jane had left, I snuck into the parlour and slipped the bag into the coffin.

The funeral was held the next day. It was a beautiful service and everyone was crying. As they closed the coffin I hoped the money was still in there.

It's all up for sale — the house, furniture, the works.

After the service the King announced he was going to take his nieces with him back to England. He wanted to hold an auction to sell the house and all the family's possessions right away.

The frauds even sold the slaves...

This is cruel.

...and thought nothing of separating families.

Are you sure you don't know where the gold is?

When the King discovered the gold was missing, he asked if I had been in his room. I lied: I said I hadn't, but I had seen one of the slaves in there just before the funeral.

I told you selling the slaves was a bad idea. Now we'll never find the gold.

The frauds were upset. *Now* they regretted selling the slaves. I was beginning to think this was going to work out for the best.

Uh, Miss Mary Jane... I got something to tell you...

I found Mary Jane in the parlour. She was unhappy over the sale of the slaves, and suddenly I wanted to tell her the truth. Since I was so used to lying, this was a new feeling for me.

Why, those evil men!

I told her the real story of the King and the Duke. As I watched her face, I was truly ashamed to think that I had been a part of their tricks.

There's someone I gotta protect.

Mary Jane wanted to have the men arrested right away. But I told her to wait, because there was someone else I needed to warn first.

That'll give me enough time to make sure my friend is safe.

Mary Jane agreed to wait till that evening to rat the frauds out.

Open it after I've gone.

I told her that I had taken the money and hidden it in a safe place. I gave her a note telling her where to find it.

You are a good boy. I shan't ever forget you.

Mary Jane thanked me, and said she would pray for me. I told her that she didn't realise the size of the promise to pray for someone like me. I never saw her again.

That afternoon the auction was held. It was sad to see...

...but at least I knew the frauds would soon be exposed.

THE PLOT UNRAVELS

Two strangers appeared at the auction – and when I heard one of them speak in an English accent, I just knew it was the real Harvey Wilks. They'd had an accident on the way – they'd lost their baggage, and the real William had broken his arm.

The scene became chaotic and no-one was sure who was who. I wanted to get out of there, but there was no escape.

The Doctor suggested that the gold ought to be held for safe keeping, but the King just laughed and said it was too late.

The real Harvey said his dead brother had a tattoo, and challenged the King to say what it was. Of course the King didn't know, so he just had to guess.

So it was decided to dig up the body. I tried to sneak off but someone grabbed a hold of me and dragged me to the cemetery.

When the coffin was opened and the gold was found, everyone started talking at once. In the confusion I slipped off and ran to find Jim. When I got to the raft I slipped and fell in the river. Before Jim could fish me out, those two frauds caught us up.

This is all your fault.

If you warn't so stupid...

The King and the Duke argued bitterly, blaming each other for losing the gold. Things weren't going to be right till we were rid of them.

As we drifted further south, we began to see Spanish moss[1] on the trees.

I wish I knew what they were up to.

The frauds made secret plans in the tepee, and Jim and I began to suspect that they were going to steal something.

One afternoon I went with the King and the Duke to a saloon. They began to argue...

Are you calling me a cheat?

You are a cheat. And a crook!

...and I saw my chance to escape.

Jim! Jim! Where are you?

But when I got to the raft, Jim was missing! I found a wanted poster that said there was a reward for a runaway slave – and then I knew those two frauds had tricked me.

Mr Phelps lives just south of town.

I ran into a boy who said that an old man had sold Jim to a Mr Phelps for $40.

Now that Jim was captured, I was overcome with guilt and shame.

I had helped a slave escape. I knew in my heart that I was a bad person.[2]

I know there ain't no hope for a sinner like me.

I tried to pray, but couldn't, so I decided to write to Miss Watson and tell her the truth.

1. Spanish moss: a plant that hangs from tree branches; it is typical of the southern United States.
2. a bad person: We know that this is not true – but Huck knows that he has broken the law.

My New Plan

But I thought of all the good times we'd had together...

I gave him my word not to tell anyone.

No – Jim and I were friends and I could never betray him, even if he was a slave.

I don't care if it is a sin — I've got to set him free.

Well there you are, boy. We was worried about you.

So I tore up the note and decided to continue my wicked ways and steal Jim out of slavery.

I put on my store-bought clothes, hid the raft upstream, and sank the canoe where I could find it later.

In town I ran into the Duke. He was posting bills for the *Royal Nonesuch* play. He pretended he was glad to see me.

I want him back.

I know where he is.

And whatever you do, don't ever tell the King I told you.

I told him I knew the truth. How could they have sold Jim for only $40?

The Duke told me that if I would keep quiet about their con, he would help me.

He said Jim was being held forty miles inland. I knew it was a lie, but I pretended to believe him.

The Phelps plantation

You dogs quit your barking, now.

As I approached the Phelps house I was suddenly surrounded by dogs. A slave woman came out to quiet them, and then Mrs Phelps appeared.

We thought you'd never get here!

She started hugging me and told me that she was my Aunt Sally. Who did she think I was?

All the way from St Petersburg, Missouri —

— our nephew, Tom Sawyer.

When Mr Silas Phelps appeared, Aunt Sally introduced me. She thought I was Tom Sawyer! I could easily go along with that.

Huck! You're alive!

Next day I ran into the real Tom Sawyer! He thought I was dead, so once again I had some explaining to do.

I wish I'd known you were rafting downriver. I'd have come with you.

I told Tom of my plan to steal Jim and help him escape. I was surprised when Tom offered to help me.

I'm much obliged for the offer, sir.

Tom appeared at the Phelps house later that day, calling himself William Thompson from Ohio, and pretending to be lost. Uncle Silas invited him to stay for supper.

Oh, Aunt Sally, it's me, Sid!

Tom accepted – and then leaned over and kissed Aunt Sally on the cheek. She turned bright red and Tom laughed, saying he was really Sid Sawyer – Tom's brother.

FINDING JIM

Looks like your friends got what was coming to them.

Tom and I went into town. We were surprised to see that the King and the Duke had been caught and had been tarred and feathered.[1] I felt a bit sorry for them.

Later we found the cabin on the Phelps plantation where Jim was being held. I suggested we steal the key and break Jim out.

All to help a slave escape!

A good plan has to be dangerous.

But this plan wasn't good enough for Tom. He offered to think up a more exciting one.

It shocked me that a respectable young man was willing to shame himself and his family just to help a slave.

It's the only honourable way to do it.

Tom's plan was to dig Jim out. That would take at least a week, but Tom was said it was the only way.

Don't worry Jim. We're gonna get you out of here.

The next morning, when Aunt Sally's slave brought Jim his breakfast, I told him that we were going to help him escape.

You have to make sure you think of everything before you start.

When I asked Tom about his plan, he said it would take weeks to work out the details. I didn't care. As long as Jim was safe, it didn't matter how long it took.

36   1. tarred and feathered: covered in hot tar and feathers as a punishment.

At first Tom said we ought to dig a moat around the cabin, and then he suggested making a saw to cut the bed Jim was chained to.

And we couldn't use shovels to dig Jim out, because the proper way was to use table knives.

It took three weeks to tunnel under the wall using knives. Tom was in his glory but I was sure there had to be an easier way.

We finished digging just in time as a gang of men were coming for Jim. We just barely escaped ahead of them.

The gang spotted us and chased us through the woods. Dogs were yapping on our trail and bullets were flying everywhere. We reached the canoe and paddled for the island where the raft was hidden.

But just as we reached the raft, a bullet pierced Tom's leg. Jim helped him onto the raft while I took the canoe and set out to find a doctor.

Next morning I ran into Uncle Silas who had been to fetch a letter for Aunt Sally.

Aunt Sally sat at the window all night long, waiting for 'Sid' to come home.

37

THE TRUTH COMES OUT

We brought your nephew, Mrs Phelps.

We oughta hang that slave for murdering this poor boy!

Before long a procession appeared carrying Tom on a mattress. The doctor and several people were with him, including Jim. Jim's hands were tied so he couldn't escape.

Aunt Sally thought he was dead, and someone in the crowd shouted that Jim was to blame.

This slave deserves our thanks for his bravery.

Oh, my poor Sid. Please don't die!

But the doctor said that Jim was a hero, and had risked his life to save Sid, instead of trying to escape.

Aunt Sally put Tom to bed and the doctor operated to remove the bullet.

What's so funny?

I just wanted the *adventure* of setting him free!

So Jim's a free man after all!

When Tom came to he confessed to helping Jim escape. But when I told him Jim was recaptured, he smiled!

Tom explained that Miss Watson had died and set Jim free in her will. He produced a letter that proved his story. So Jim had been free all along! I wondered why Tom hadn't said something before.

Hello, Sally. Didn't you get my letter?

Suddenly, Tom's Aunt Polly appeared. My heart skipped a beat as I tried to find a place to hide.

I slid under the bed.

We're in deep trouble now.

This isn't Sid. It's Tom Sawyer.

But if this is Tom, then who is...?

Aunt Sally was delighted to see her sister, and recounted Sid's bravery when the gang was after Jim. But Aunt Polly set things straight as to who was who, and our hoax was finally revealed.

Aunt Polly had written to Aunt Sally several times, but Tom had hidden the letters so he wouldn't be found out.

It's true, Jim. You're a free man at last!

Then she confirmed that Miss Watson had set Jim free in her will. Jim was jubilant, and Tom was so happy that he gave Jim $40 of his own money.

I'll light out for the Territories.[1]

I asked Tom what he wanted to do next. He was planning to go out West, but I think Aunt Polly had other ideas.

Jim had some bad news for me.

He was my only family.

But I know I'm better off without him.

Remember that dead man we found in the floating house?

That was your Pap.

Yours truly, Huck Finn.

So that's my story. It was a lot of trouble writing this book – and now I'm done I'm going to light out for the Territories. Aunt Sally's talking about adopting me and trying to 'sivilize'[2] me, and I can't stand it – I been there before.

1. the Territories: the lands in the West that had not yet become states.
2. sivilize: Huck's way of spelling 'civilise'.

THE END

Mark Twain was the pen name of Samuel Langhorne Clemens, an American author and humorist who wrote novels, plays, short stories and essays addressing his views on post-Civil War society. He is often referred to as 'the father of American literature', as he was the first author to write about real American themes and the first to use the everyday language of common people. His best-known and most controversial work, *Adventures of Huckleberry Finn*, has been called the first great American novel.

Mark Twain on board a Mississippi steamboat.

EARLY LIFE

Samuel Clemens was born in Florida, Missouri in 1835. In 1839, when he was four years old, the family moved to Hannibal, Missouri, a town on the Mississippi River. Hannibal was the model for the fictional St Petersburg, which is the setting for *The Adventures of Tom Sawyer* and the starting point for *Huckleberry Finn*.

Young Sam began writing at the age of twelve, when he was apprenticed to his brother Orion as a typesetter for the *Hannibal Journal*, a local newspaper. For the next eleven years he perfected his writing skills while spending many hours reading in public libraries in an effort to complete his limited education.

TRAVELLING AND WRITING

In 1857 the eighteen-year-old Sam became fascinated with steamboat travel, and spent four years training to become a riverboat pilot. It was at this time that he devised his famous pen name. 'Mark twain' was the shout of the linesman testing the depth of the river – it meant that two fathoms (twelve feet or 3.77 metres) of water had been 'marked', or measured. ('Twain' is an old-fashioned word for 'two'.) His experiences as a cub riverboat pilot were the basis of his book *Life on the Mississippi*, which was published in 1883.

In 1861, Twain joined his brother Orion on a stagecoach trip to Nevada, which he wrote about in his 1872 book *Roughing It*. Twain spent some time living in silver-mining camps and working for a local newspaper, before moving to San Francisco, where he began writing short stories. His best-known story, 'The Celebrated Jumping

Frog of Calaveras County', published in 1865, made him famous, and the thirty-year-old Twain began a new career as a travelling lecturer and humorist.

MARRIAGE AND FAMILY

In 1870 Twain married Olivia Langdon (1845–1904), and the next year they built a house in Hartford, Connecticut. The couple had three daughters, Susy, Clara, and Jean, and a son, Langdon, but Jean was the only one who outlived her parents. The early deaths of his other children affected Twain's writing in later years.

INTERNATIONAL FAME

In Hartford Mark Twain wrote many of his most famous novels, including *Tom Sawyer* and *Huckleberry Finn*, as well as *Life on the Mississippi*, which is said to have been the first book ever composed on a typewriter. Twain was fascinated with technology – he invested heavily in a typesetting machine and lost most of his fortune when it turned out to be a failure. In later years he took to the lecture circuit again, and was able to recoup some of his lost fortune from speaking engagements.

Mark Twain received an honorary Doctor of Letters degree from Yale University in 1901, and a second honorary doctorate from Oxford University in 1907.

THE END

In 1835, the year Mark Twain was born, Halley's Comet was visible in the night sky. Twain often said he would 'go out' with the comet when it appeared again in 1910. In 1909 he wrote, 'The Almighty has said, no doubt: "Now here are these two unaccountable freaks; they came in together, they must go out together."' Sure enough, Twain died of a heart attack on 21 April 1910 in Redding, Connecticut.

The library at Mark Twain's house in Hartford, Connecticut.

Look out for me, oh muddy water.
Your mysteries are deep and wide,
And I got a need for going some place,
And I got a need to climb upon your back and ride.

(from 'Muddy Water' by Roger Miller,
from the Broadway musical *Big River*)

The Mississippi River has always been an important part of American culture and history. The river was central to many Native American legends, and has been written about in poetry, plays, short stories, novels and songs. Native Americans called the river the 'Father of Waters', and the waterway has had many nicknames – Big Muddy, the Mighty Mississippi, Moon River, Old Man River, Ol' Miss, and the Big River. In *Life on the Mississippi*, Mark Twain refers to the river as both 'the Body of the Nation' and a 'Great Sewer'. Geography books often call the Mississippi 'the backbone of America'.

It is hard to measure a river exactly, and estimates of the Mississippi's length vary from 3,780 km (2,350 miles) to 4,025 km (just over 2,500 miles). This makes the Mississippi either the longest or the second-longest river in North America, although at 6,920 km (over 4,300 miles) in length the combined Mississippi–Missouri River system is the longest in the world. The Mississippi River watershed drains 3.4 million square km (almost 1.3 million square miles) – nearly half the landmass of the continental United States.

EXPLORATION

The first European to sail up the Mississippi was the Spanish adventurer Hernando de Soto in 1541, but it was the French who systematically explored the river, starting in the 1670s with the travels of Louis Joliet and Jacques Marquette. The Mississippi became an important means of travel for French fur trappers, who used the river system to trade with Native American tribes.

After the American Revolution the Mississippi became the western boundary of the newly independent United States, and within twenty years westward expansion brought the Americans into conflict with both the French and the Spanish. With no roads other than Native trails, the rivers were the only effective means of transport in the West. The city of New Orleans – founded near the mouth of the river in 1718 – was fast becoming the most important port in North America. In 1803 President Thomas Jefferson offered to buy New Orleans from the French, who surprised Jefferson by offering to sell all of the Louisiana Territory to the United States for $15 million. This 'Louisiana Purchase' effectively doubled the size of the nation.

MISSISSIPPI RIVERBOATS

The development of the steamboat helped establish the Mississippi River system as the major highway of pre-Civil War America. Farmers would use the river to bring their goods to market, and vessels of all sizes and descriptions could be found on the Mississippi, carrying grains, fruits and vegetables, livestock, firewood, whisky, and manufactured goods. In addition, the river was essential to the plantation economy of the South. In the nineteenth century, millions of bales of cotton travelled along the Mighty Mississippi to New Orleans, which was the largest cotton-exporting city in the world. Even the coming of the railways did not reduce the importance of the waterway, which is still used today as a major shipping channel.

But for most people the river conjures up romantic images of steamboats, flatboats and rafts, as well as riverboat gamblers, jazz musicians, travelling minstrel shows, and the uniquely American idea that opportunity is just around the corner – or the next bend in the river.

Mississippi steamboats racing, 1859. Note the raft in the foreground.

43

Perhaps the greatest influence on Mark Twain's writings was his experience of growing up in Missouri in pre-Civil War America. Both *Tom Sawyer* and *Adventures of Huckleberry Finn* draw closely on his boyhood memories.

Admitted to the Union in 1821, Missouri was a Slave State. (Under United States law at this time, there were some states where slavery was legal and others where it was not.) Although not everyone in Missouri believed that slavery should be tolerated, many white people held that blacks were socially and intellectually inferior. Young Samuel Clemens grew up in an environment that treated all blacks, free or enslaved, as objects of ridicule and distrust.

HUCK'S DILEMMA

Like Mark Twain himself, Huck Finn was brought up in a society that thought slavery was both right and natural. When Huck runs away from his father, he is seeking freedom; and when he meets Jim on Jackson's Island, he is surprised to find that Jim has run away from Miss Watson for the same reason – freedom. Huck struggles with a moral dilemma: he knows he is breaking the law by helping a runaway slave, yet he slowly begins to see Jim as a fellow human being, and a friend. He is confused, because this goes against all he has been taught about slaves.

To add to his confusion, Miss Watson has constantly told young Huck that he lacks moral character and judgement. In the end, when Huck decides to do the right thing and help Jim escape, he believes he is doing wrong, and that Miss Watson was right about his lack of character.

CONTROVERSY

Huckleberry Finn is one of the most controversial books in American literature. The first efforts to have the book banned came in 1885 – the year after it was published – as many white Americans objected to the theme of friendship between white and black. Since then the book has raised concerns from various groups who have objected to the relationship between thirteen-year-old Huck and the older Jim, the violence of Southern society, the child abuse that Huck suffers at the hands of his father, and the cruelty of slavery.

The book has drawn reactions from people who object to Huck's hatred of school, his willingness to abandon settled society for the vagabond life of the river, and even the corncob pipe he smokes – a device Twain uses to show differences in social class and Huck's lack of 'proper' upbringing. In recent years, opposition to *Huckleberry Finn* has come increasingly from African Americans who find the negative images of blacks and the language of the story offensive. Today the book is banned in many American schools, and until recently it was consistently listed in the top ten banned books by the American Library Association.

Yet *Huckleberry Finn* is widely read around the world and is taught in a majority of American high schools. It was recently listed by the *Great Books Guide* as one of the hundred greatest novels ever written.

HISTORY OF AMERICAN SLAVERY

Slavery existed in the Americas from 1501 when the first African slaves were brought to Santo Domingo (in the present-day Dominican Republic) until 1888 when Brazil abolished slavery. It is estimated that at least twelve million slaves were brought from Africa between 1501 and 1808 when the transatlantic slave trade was abolished – although the slave trade flourished illegally for many years afterwards.

1501
Spanish bring first African slaves to the New World.

1519
Portuguese import slaves into Brazil to work on sugar plantations. At least 75% of all slaves brought to the New World would be employed in growing and processing sugar.

1619
First slaves brought to Jamestown, Virginia.

1662–1705
Southern colonies pass laws making slavery hereditary and defining slaves as chattels (personal property).

1775
First abolitionist society formed in Philadelphia.

1775–1783
Revolutionary War. Thousands of American slaves enlist in the Continental Army, on the promise of freedom at the end of the war.

1780s
The states of Connecticut, New Hampshire, Rhode Island and Massachusetts pass laws limiting or abolishing slavery.

1790s–1865
The Underground Railroad – a secret network of escape routes and safe houses – helps tens of thousands of runaway slaves to escape.

1793
US Congress passes Fugitive Slave Act. Helping an escaped slave is now a federal crime.

1794
Eli Whitney's cotton gin makes large-scale cultivation of cotton profitable.

1807
England outlaws transatlantic slave trade.

1808
United States outlaws transatlantic slave trade.

1833
American Anti-Slavery Society founded.

1839
Mutiny on the slave ship *Amistad* draws attention to the illegal slave trade in Cuba.

1852
Harriet Beecher Stowe publishes her best-selling anti-slavery novel *Uncle Tom's Cabin*.

1861–1865
American Civil War.

1863
President Abraham Lincoln issues Emancipation Proclamation, freeing all slaves in rebel states and territories.

1865
Thirteenth Amendment to the US Constitution abolishes slavery in the United States.

1867: *The Celebrated Jumping Frog of Calaveras County*. 27 short stories.

1869: *Innocents Abroad*. A collection of letters written during a five-month tour of Europe, the Middle East and North Africa.

1872: *Roughing It*. Autobiographical account of Twain's five years in Nevada and California.

1873: *The Gilded Age*. Satire of greed and political corruption in post-Civil War America, co-authored with Charles Dudley Warner.

1875: *The Adventures of Tom Sawyer*. Fictional version of Twain's boyhood in Hannibal, Missouri.

1880: *A Tramp Abroad*. Twain's second travel book details a sixteen-month stay in Europe.

1881: *The Prince and the Pauper*. Historical novel set in 1547. Presents a fictionalised account of mistaken identity and events leading up to the coronation of English king Edward VI.

1883: *Excerpts from Adam's Diary*. Twain satirises religion and American society.

1883: *Life on the Mississippi*. Twain's account of his years as an apprentice riverboat pilot.

1884: *Adventures of Huckleberry Finn*. Combines elements of *Tom Sawyer* and *Life on the Mississippi* with strong anti-slavery theme as well as satire of Southern society.

1889: *A Connecticut Yankee in King Arthur's Court*. Twain's second historical novel is really an early science-fiction story about time travel and how modern technology might have affected life in the Middle Ages.

1894: *Pudd'nhead Wilson*. Twain's last fictional work addresses issues of race and class in American society.

1896: *Personal Recollections of Joan of Arc*. Historical novel about the life of Saint Joan.

1897: *Following the Equator*. Twain's account of a worldwide lecture tour.

1897: *How to Tell a Story and Other Essays*. Twain discusses his own writing style.

1905: *Eve's Diary*. More satire in the vein of *Adam's Diary*.

1909: *Excerpts from Captain Stormfield's Visit to Heaven*. Originally written in the 1860s, this story is Twain's most biting satire of American life.

1924: *The Autobiography of Mark Twain*. Published after the author's death, as Twain said, 'to protect the guilty', revised in 1959.

1935: *Mark Twain's Notebook*. Twain's edited notebooks provide insight into his ideas and writings.

1962: *Letters From the Earth*. Written in 1909, these essays continue Twain's themes of religious and social satire.

STAGE AND SCREEN

ADAPTATIONS OF *HUCKLEBERRY FINN*

Huckleberry Finn is a classic story of the human desire for freedom, and the image of Jim and Huck sailing lazily down the Mississippi River is one that captures the imagination of all people seeking to escape from the problems of everyday life. Huck is a Peter Pan-like character – the perennial thirteen-year-old who finds that friendship and love are all that really matter in life. Huck Finn is one of the most popular images in American literature, and the character has been portrayed in movies, plays and animated films around the world.

FILM ADAPTATIONS OF *HUCKLEBERRY FINN*

1937: *Huck Finn*, Paramount Pictures.

1939: *The Adventures of Huckleberry Finn*, starring Mickey Rooney.

1960: *The Adventures of Huckleberry Finn*, starring Eddie Hodges.

1968: *The New Adventures of Huckleberry Finn*, animated television series.

1972: *Hopelessly Lost* (USSR).

1974: *Huckleberry Finn*, musical.

1975: *Huckleberry Finn*, musical starring Ron Howard.

1976: *Huckleberry no Bouken*, Japanese anime series.

1979: *Huckleberry Finn and His Friends*, television series starring Ian Tracey.

1985: *Adventures of Huckleberry Finn*, television movie (pictured above right).

1993: *The Adventures of Huck Finn*, starring Elijah Wood and Courtney B. Vance.

STAGE PRODUCTIONS

1985: *Big River*, Broadway musical with lyrics and music by Roger Miller.

FILMS ABOUT MARK TWAIN

1944: *The Adventures of Mark Twain*, Warner Brothers.

1967: *Mark Twain Tonight*, television movie starring Hal Holbrook, based on a 1966 Tony Award-winning play.

1985: *The Adventures of Mark Twain*, Harbor Towns (Claymation).

2001: *Mark Twain: A Film by Ken Burns*, Corporation for Public Broadcasting.

INDEX

A

Adventures of Huckleberry Finn 40, 41, 44, 47
Adventures of Tom Sawyer 40, 41, 44

C

'Celebrated Jumping Frog of Calaveras County' 40–41
Clemens, Orion 40
Clemens, Samuel Langhorne *see* Twain, Mark

F

films 47
Florida, Missouri 40

H

Halley's Comet 41
Hannibal, Missouri 40
Hartford, Connecticut 41

J

Jefferson, Thomas, US President 42

L

Langdon, Olivia 41
Life on the Mississippi 40, 41
Louisiana Purchase 42

M

Missouri
 (river) 40, 42–43
 (state) 40, 44

N

Nevada 40
New Orleans, Louisiana 42, 43

P

plays 47

R

Redding, Connecticut 41
Roughing It 40

S

San Francisco, California 40
slavery 44–45
steamboats 40, 43

T

Twain, Mark 40–41, 44, 47
 children 41
 works 46

IF YOU LIKED THIS BOOK, YOU MIGHT LIKE TO TRY THESE OTHER GRAFFEX TITLES:

Dracula Bram Stoker
Dr Jekyll and Mr Hyde Robert Louis Stevenson
Frankenstein Mary Shelley
The Hunchback of Notre Dame Victor Hugo
Journey to the Centre of the Earth Jules Verne
Kidnapped Robert Louis Stevenson
Macbeth William Shakespeare

The Man in the Iron Mask Alexandre Dumas
Moby-Dick Herman Melville
Oliver Twist Charles Dickens
A Tale of Two Cities Charles Dickens
The Three Musketeers Alexandre Dumas
Treasure Island Robert Louis Stevenson

FOR MORE INFORMATION ON MARK TWAIN:

The Official Website of Mark Twain: http://www.cmgww.com/historic/twain/
The Mark Twain House: http://www.marktwainhouse.org/
The Literature Network: http://www.online-literature.com/twain/
PBS: Mark Twain by Ken Burns: http://www.pbs.org/marktwain/
Huckleberry Finn Resources, University of Virginia:
  http://etext.virginia.edu/twain/huckfinn.html